THE TOTALLY INCREDIBLE BOOK OF UNBELIEVABLE FACTS

AUTUMN
PUBLISHING

Produced by Tall Tree Books
Written by Katie Dicker
Cover designed by Richard Sykes
Designed by Richard Sykes and Jonathon Vipond
Edited by Rebecca Kealy

Published in 2023
First published in the UK by Autumn Publishing
An imprint of Igloo Books Ltd
Cottage Farm, NN6 0BJ, UK
Owned by Bonnier Books
Sveavägen 56, Stockholm, Sweden

Manufactured in China. 0823 001
10 9 8 7 6 5 4 3 2 1

Library of Congress Cataloging-in-Publication
Data is available upon request.

ISBN 978-1-83771-684-5
autumnpublishing.co.uk
bonnierbooks.co.uk

THE TOTALLY INCREDIBLE BOOK OF UNBELIEVABLE FACTS

AUTUMN PUBLISHING

CONTENTS

SPACE RACE

SUPER TECH

BRILLIANT BODY

PAST TIMES

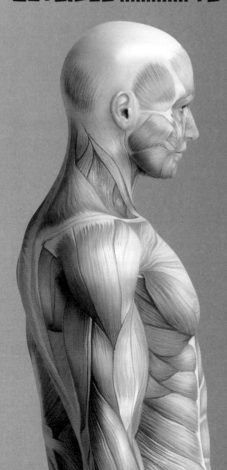

PRECIOUS PLANET

AWESOME ANIMALS

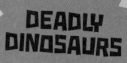

DEADLY DINOSAURS

SPACE RACE

Our desire to learn more about the Universe has revealed some incredible discoveries. From telescopes and space probes to rockets and rovers, hold tight as we take you on a trip that's out of this world!

page 8

FORCE OF NATURE

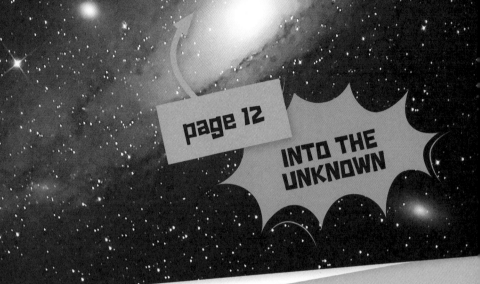

FORCE OF NATURE

Our solar system is filled with big and beautiful objects!

The Sun makes up **99.68 percent** of the total mass of our solar system.

The Sun

RISING STAR

The Sun is the only star in our solar system. Its gravity holds the entire thing together.

It is so huge that it would take a passenger jet six months to fly around the Sun—or if you went by bike, 28 years!

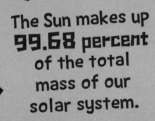

The Sun is such a big ball of gas, more than a **million Earths** could fit inside it!

FIRST BORN

Our solar system formed about 4.5 billion years ago.

The oldest planet is Jupiter. Its mass is about 1,000 times smaller than the Sun, but that's still more than twice the mass of all the other planets combined!

Jupiter

Io

Ganymede

Saturn

MANY MOONS AGO

There are 176 known moons in our solar system—Saturn and Jupiter both have about 80!

Scientists think Earth's moon formed when Earth collided with a smaller planet, about 4.5 billion years ago.

Jupiter's largest moon, Ganymede, is bigger than the planet Mercury! The most active moon is Jupiter's Io, which has hundreds of volcanoes erupting every second.

The Moon's orbit used to be 10 times closer to Earth, but every year it moves about **1.5 inches** further away.

FREAKY FACT!
Venus spins so slowly on its axis, that one day there is longer than the time it takes to orbit the Sun!

WHO KNEW?

Venus and Uranus are the only two planets in our solar system that spin clockwise.

While it takes Uranus about 17 Earth hours to complete one rotation, it takes Venus 243 Earth days!

FLYING DEBRIS

Look out—our solar system is full of hidden dangers, too!

ROCKY PATCH

It's not just planets that orbit the Sun in our solar system.

Asteroids are pieces of rock, mostly found in the "asteroid belt" between Mars and Jupiter. Jupiter's gravity sometimes nudges them into a different orbit, sending them on a collision course with Earth.

DINO DESTROYER!
When a **9-mile-wide** asteroid hit Earth **66** million years ago, it wiped out **70** percent of species on Earth, including the dinosaurs!

WHAT ARE METEORS?

Collisions can cause small pieces of asteroids and comets to travel toward Earth as meteoroids.

If these meteoroids enter Earth's atmosphere at high speed, they burn up and we see them as shooting stars (meteors). Any that survive, fall to the ground as meteorites.

FROZEN GIANTS

Comets orbit the Sun, too.

When these frozen balls of ice and dust get close to the Sun, they start to vaporize. This produces a huge glowing head with long tails that stream behind.

HOW DO COMETS SMELL?

In 2014, a space probe landed on a comet for the first time—and that's how we know they smell bad (a bit like cat pee or rotten eggs!).

The word comet comes from the Greek "kometes" (long hair) because their tails stretch for millions of miles.

Meteorite particles have been found to be **5-7 billion years old!** That's older than the solar system itself.

This large crater in Arizona, USA, was formed when a meteorite slammed into the ground some 50,000 years ago.

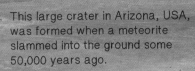

AVERTING DISASTER

In 2013, a meteor the size of a house entered Earth's atmosphere at about 42,690 mph and exploded.

The shockwave was up to 30 times the power of the Hiroshima bomb (see page 55). It knocked people right off their feet, damaged buildings, and injured over 1,600 people.

This is one of the last pictures taken by DART before it hit the asteroid.

Scientists are always monitoring objects heading in our direction and developing lifesaving strategies. In 2022, they sent the DART spacecraft crashing into an asteroid to change its orbit!

INTO THE UNKNOWN

What lies beyond our solar system is out of this world!

WHAT IS THE OORT CLOUD?

The Oort Cloud is the edge of our solar system.

Scientists think that icy objects, like comets, orbit the Sun here.

Sometimes, collisions here or the gravitational pull of another object can knock a comet off course, sending it toward the Sun.

LONG ORBITS
Some objects in the Oort Cloud can take hundreds of thousands of years to orbit the Sun.

From Earth, the Milky Way looks like a milky band stretching right across the night sky.

MILKY WAY TO GO!

Scientists think there may be a hundred billion galaxies in the whole Universe!

Our solar system is part of a galaxy called the Milky Way, which has about 200-400 billion stars.

The closest large galaxy is the Andromeda Galaxy. On a dark, moonless night, you may just see it as a faint, starry cloud in the sky.

YOU CAN'T BE SIRIUS!

Sirius is the brightest star in the night sky, although it takes nearly nine years for its light to reach our eyes.

If Sirius was placed next to the Sun, it would be twice as huge and over 20 times brighter!

The Sun

Sirius

DID YOU KNOW?
Sirius is also known as the "dog star" because it is part of the constellation Canis Major, which means "the greater dog."

NEARLY NEIGHBORS?
The Andromeda Galaxy is about **21 million trillion** miles away!

SUPER STARS

Scientists think there are more stars in the Universe than grains of sand on Earth's beaches!

While we don't know exactly how many there are of either, they've estimated that there are about a septillion stars (1 with 24 zeros) in the whole Universe, and about 7.5 quintillion (7.5 with 18 zeros) grains of sand on Earth's beaches.

CLOSER INSPECTION

From telescopes to space probes, we're finding out more than ever before!

GRANTECAN

The largest telescope on Earth is found on La Palma in the Canary Islands.

Gran Telescopio Canarias (or "GranTeCan") uses a 34 foot mirror made up of 36 hexagonal segments to collect and focus light.

LONG VISION
GranTeCan is so powerful, it can capture images from galaxies millions of light years away.

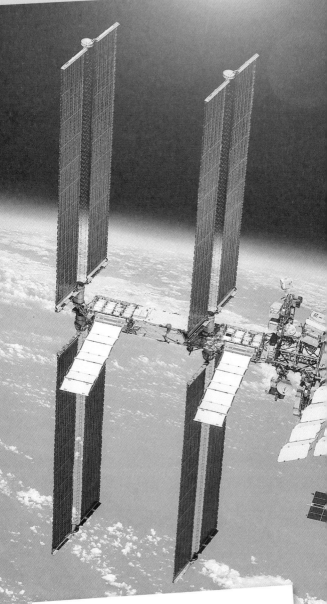

THE ISS

The International Space Station (ISS) is the largest man-made object in space.

JAMES WEBB TELESCOPE

When it was launched in 2021, the James Webb Space Telescope was so big that it had to be folded inside its rocket launcher. It took a total of 30 years to develop!

About 100 times more powerful than the 1990 Hubble Space Telescope, the James Webb hopes to capture images of the very first galaxies—about 13.5 billion light years away.

MIRROR, MIRROR
The James Webb Telescope's **21 foot** mirror is made up of **18** hexagonal segments, each coated in a layer of gold. And its **75 foot** sunshield is about the length of a tennis court.

VOYAGER 1

CALLING EARTH
Radio signals take about **22 hours** to reach Voyager 1!

About 15 space probes are exploring our Universe as you read this!

Voyager 1 is the most distant probe, now about 14 billion miles from Earth, traveling at an amazing 38,000 mph (a passenger jet usually cruises at 550 mph).

It would take Voyager 1 about 300 years to reach the Oort Cloud, and another 30,000 to fly beyond it.

Assembled in orbit, it's 120 yards long (about the length of a soccer field) and weighs 900,000 lbs, which is more than 300 cars.

Astronauts have been living and working on this research station since 2000.

SPEEDY ORBIT
Positioned **250 miles** from Earth, the ISS takes **1.5 hours** to circle our planet, at a speed of **17,000 mph**.

SPACE TRAVEL

Who knows what the future holds?

SEEING THE SIGHTS

Many scientists think that space tourism could flourish in the future, but at a cost.

$20-40 million can already get you a trip to the ISS!

If you have $10 billion to spare, one day you might be able to spend a weekend at a space hotel.

Some companies are even planning day trips in a balloon-lifted spacecraft, so visitors can see the curvature of our planet—but seats will cost you at least $50,000.

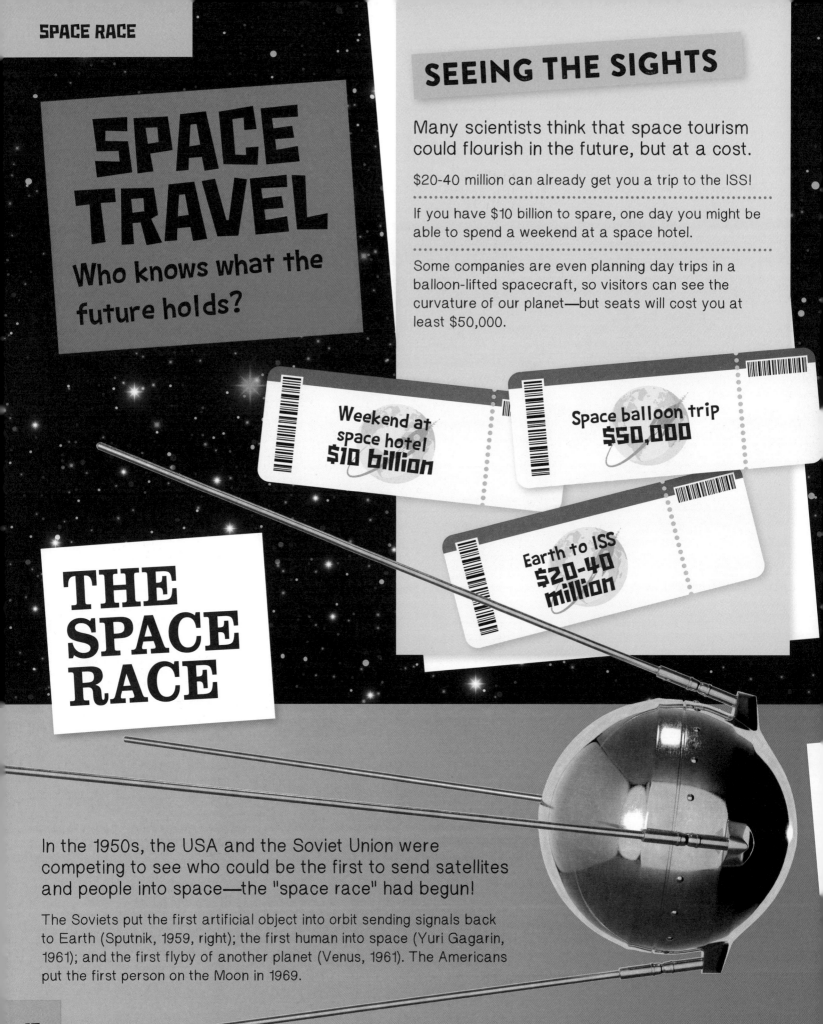

Weekend at
space hotel
$10 billion

Space balloon trip
$50,000

Earth to ISS
$20-40
million

THE SPACE RACE

In the 1950s, the USA and the Soviet Union were competing to see who could be the first to send satellites and people into space—the "space race" had begun!

The Soviets put the first artificial object into orbit sending signals back to Earth (Sputnik, 1959, right); the first human into space (Yuri Gagarin, 1961); and the first flyby of another planet (Venus, 1961). The Americans put the first person on the Moon in 1969.

ROBOTIC VEHICLES

Space rovers have been exploring Mars for years!

In 2021, Perseverance became the fifth rover to land on Mars. Its mission is to collect soil and rock samples, and to look for signs of ancient life.

It joins Curiosity, which has been exploring Mars for more than a decade, finding evidence of past water, and environmental changes.

Perseverance carried a small helicopter to Mars too, called Ingenuity.

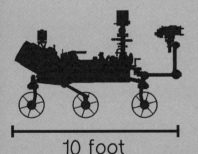

10 foot

ROBOT CAR
Perseverance is a wheeled vehicle about **10 foot** long and weighing about **2,260 lbs**, making it the size of a small car!

LIFE IN SPACE

Which way is down?

Astronauts need to adapt to the unique conditions found in space.

On Earth, the pull of gravity keeps our bones and muscles constantly working to support us. In the zero gravity of space, however, astronauts must exercise regularly to keep their bones and muscles functioning properly. They do this by using treadmills, exercise bikes, and weightlifting machines.

STAR SAILOR
The word astronaut comes from the Greek "astron nautes," meaning star sailor.

SUPER TECH

The world of technology changes so fast! Humans can fly, robots save lives, and body parts can be printed. From megabits to molecular medicine, let's take a tour of all things tech.

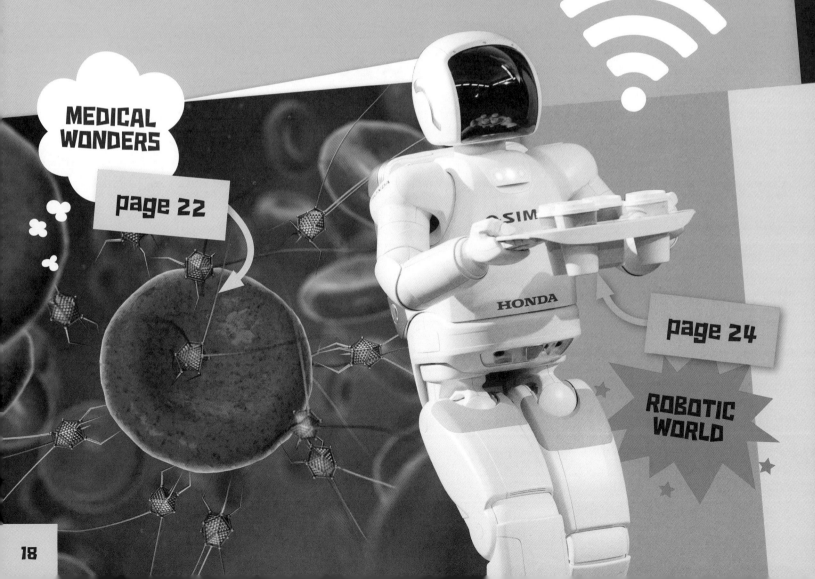

VIRTUAL LIVIN'

REAL LIFE SCI-FI

REVOLUTIONARY RIDES

EVER CHANGING

With regular updates and big breakthroughs, there's always something new to learn!

DID YOU KNOW?
In 2020, the latest smartphone was about **900 million times** faster than the computer used to guide the Apollo 11 moon landing in 1969.

SUPER GROWTH

Our world is changing all the time, and technology is no exception.

Every day, about 3.5 million terabytes of data is produced—as photos, videos, sound, and text—and global data is expected to reach 175 billion terabytes by 2025.

For scale, a desktop computer has about 2 terabytes of storage. Thankfully, the speed of technology is keeping up with demand.

DATA TRANSFER

In 2009, a pigeon carrying a memory stick was found to be twice as fast as South Africa's broadband service.

The pigeon delivered the memory stick and the data in just over an hour, while the broadband took over two hours to transfer 4GB of data.

Now, the global average speed is about 34 megabits per second (Mbps).

I can't keep up with that!

Iceland currently has the fastest broadband speed with an average of 216.56 Mbps. At that speed, you could download the same file as the carrier pigeon in about 2.5 minutes.

SUPER SEARCHER
Google is currently the world's fastest search engine, receiving over **99,000** searches a second and using more than **1,000** machines to retrieve an answer in **0.2 seconds.**

Google

KEEPING CONNECTED

We've all gotten used to wireless devices thanks to WiFi—radio waves that transfer electronic information from one device to another. But there's almost always that one room in a house that struggles to connect to the WiFi.

Well what about this for a long-distance signal? In 2002, an experiment by the Swedish Space Corporation used a wireless network connection to link devices that were almost 200 miles apart!

HEAD IN THE CLOUDS

Cloud servers help us to keep up with the demand for data, and let us access information over the Internet wherever we are.

One of the world's biggest data centers is found in Nevada, USA. It has about **7.2 million square foot** of server space (that's about **2,500 tennis courts**) and gets its power from local solar and wind farms.

MEDICAL WONDERS

Technology is helping change the future of medicine, too!

THE MASSPEC PEN

In 2017, clinical trials of a pen-like device helped surgeons to distinguish healthy cells from cancerous tissue within seconds!

The MasSpec Pen can help surgeons to make decisions on the spot, rather than waiting for laboratory tests, and is now being developed for wider use.

The tests showed that the MasSpec Pen had an overall accuracy of **96.3 percent.**

NANOTECH

Nanotechnology could help doctors to find, guide medicine toward, and destroy cells showing early signs of cancer.

These small nanoparticles are no bigger than a billionth of a meter, but scientists think that robots as small as 100 billionths of a meter could be used to explore and treat the inside of a blood cell.

Nanobots could be used to examine a red blood cell.

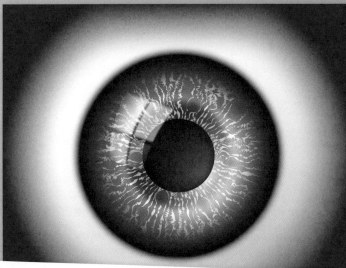

SOUND AND SIGHT

Scientists believe they could also use nanoparticles in the eye to absorb light and send signals to the brain. This could restore sight in patients with diseases of the retina, the light-sensitive part at the back of the eye.

Wireless technology has also improved the quality of hearing aids. These can now be used together on each ear, rather than separately as they once would, to improve the quality of signals sent to the brain.

SPEECH REVIVAL

In 2021, technology helped a paralyzed man to speak in sentences again by translating signals from his brain into text on a computer screen.

While previous systems required patients to "type" words, letter by letter, this patient was simply able to imagine saying the words.

DID YOU KNOW?
A computer can convert text into speech. And if past samples of a person's voice are available, their tone and accent can be used, too!

ROBOTIC WORLD

Will robots ever rule the world?

LIVING DOLL

In 2017, Sophia, the world's most lifelike and intelligent robot, was given citizenship in Saudi Arabia.

Sophia can walk freely and her face of artificial skin is so lifelike, she can also copy emotional responses.

More than 60 facial and neck mechanisms create these real life movements.

I can even speak 38 different languages.

Sophia is also able to learn and adapt to different conversations.

LIFESAVERS

Four-legged robot dogs have been designed to work in high risk areas that are too dangerous for humans.

They can enter high radiation zones and badly damaged buildings, move on scattered debris, and squeeze through narrow gaps to search for people who are trapped.

HELPING HAND

Before Sophia, there was ASIMO ("Advanced Step in Innovative Mobility").

Created in 2000 and standing 4 ft 1 in tall (about the height of a seated adult), ASIMO could climb stairs, walk backward, hop, kick a ball, and even open a bottle and pour a drink.

ASIMO was also able to recognize voices and faces, and to respond to gestures and commands.

ASIMO retired in 2022 so its developers could work on more practical projects, such as robots that care for the elderly, or assist with disaster relief.

Just don't ask me to play fetch!

IDEAL AID!

Robots are increasingly becoming a part of our lives.

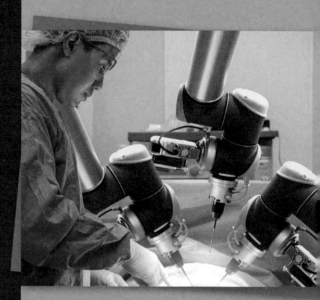

Doctor and robot performing surgery. Sometimes, the robots can be operated by a surgeon who isn't even inside the operating room.

A robot navigating a sidewalk to deliver a package. Robots can also inspect machinery, guide blind people, and serve in restaurants. They don't need any sleep, they have infinite memories, and they're good at multi-tasking. Sounds like an ideal candidate!

VIRTUAL LIVIN'

From computer gaming to the Metaverse—it's life, but not as we know it!

VR can let you tour the surface of another Planet!

TOUCHY FEELY
A vibrating body suit can also give you the sensation of the 3D objects you touch!

VIRTUAL REALITY (VR)

VR allows you to explore simulations of reality. The devices often come with a headset to see and hear the virtual world, and controllers that you can use to move and perform actions.

But with more advanced VR, you can literally walk around your virtual world using robotic boots, or even specialized treadmills!

While VR video games are most common, the devices can also be used to help train surgeons and pilots safely.

TOUR IN A HEADSET

Virtual reality is making it easier to explore than ever before.

With VR, you can tour famous sights from the comfort of your own home! From live concerts to sporting events—put the headset on and you can really feel as if you're part of the crowd.

VIRTUAL PAST
Some museums and historical societies now use VR headsets to show visitors what ancient sites looked like in the past.

AUGMENTED REALITY (AR)

While virtual reality replaces the real world, AR provides a "mixed reality" experience, so you can stay firmly rooted in the real world.

AR smart glasses, for example, could give extra information when you look at a historic building, or a shopping app on your smartphone can help you to visualize furniture in your own home.

Scientists are even developing AR contact lenses that offer the same benefits—as a completely hands-free device!

THE METAVERSE

The Metaverse is a virtual reality world that allows us to meet friends, family, teachers, and colleagues, even when we're physically apart.

You can create an Avatar—an electronic version of yourself—to move around and interact in a virtual world with friends all over the planet!

REAL LIFE SCI-FI

When fiction becomes reality . . .

REAL LIFE SUPERHEROES!

The long sought-after dream of human flight has become a reality thanks to the jet pack! This is a backpack that uses jet engines to push the wearer into the air.

In 2019, British inventor Richard Browning set a new speed record of over 85 mph while wearing a jet-engine-powered suit!

Up, up, and away!

HOLOGRAPHIC WORLD

Sci-fi films rely on special effects like holograms, but these virtual images are now making a mark in the real world.

Hologram mannequins in shops can bring clothes to life. Hologram patients can be used in medical training. And hologram personal trainers can make you sweat like there's no tomorrow!

DRONES ON DUTY

Real life flying robots!

Drones are becoming increasingly important in the modern world. They can even work independently, navigating through the sky and "consciously" avoiding any possible collisions.

Hospitals can use drones to deliver medical supplies to remote areas and to those affected by war.

Drones can reach and photograph inaccessible places, to help identify structural damage in buildings, or diseased crops in agricultural land.

DID YOU KNOW?
Scientists can even 3D print coral reefs using terracotta clay. The clay gives algae a place to grow to hopefully rebuild endangered reefs.

3D PRINTERS

The first 3D printers used plastics and resins, but developing technology can now manufacture human tissue, organ parts, blood, and bones!

3D printing can create custom-made designs, such as artificial limbs, and lifelike models can be created to practice surgery.

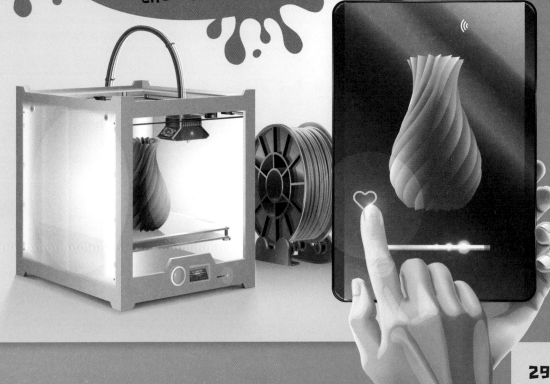

REVOLUTIONARY RIDES

From record breakers of the past to the future of travel ...

DID YOU KNOW?
The SR-71 plane had a titanium alloy coating to allow it to cope with temperatures up to **590 °F.**

SUPER SOARER

The world's fastest jet aircraft was the Lockheed SR-71 Blackbird.

Its top speed was over 2,175 mph, which is more than three times the speed of sound. It was used for surveillance and could cover up to 62 sq m in an hour.

OIL GIANT

The *Seawise Giant* oil tanker held the record for the biggest ship.

Twice the size of the *Titanic*, it had a deck the size of the Lincoln Memorial Reflecting Pool.

It took almost 5 miles to come to a halt from full speed and was too long to sail through the shallow waters of the English Channel or the Suez and Panama Canals.

When it was scrapped in 2010, it took 18,000 workers to dismantle it.

1,640 foot

FLOATING MONSTER
The ship was almost **1,640 foot** long, which is greater than the height of the Empire State building!

SKY'S THE LIMIT

Aerial taxi services could exist sooner than you think, to help link cities to local airports or residential areas.

Powered with lithium-ion batteries (like electric cars) for zero emissions, they will be able to take off and land vertically, meaning small "skyports" could handle around 1,000 landings an hour. The technology aims to reduce commuter times and to ease traffic congestion.

Pilots wore special pressure suits to withstand the extreme conditions.

Driverless cars are already being used in some parts of the world for taxi services and pizza deliveries!

SILENT CHAUFFEUR

In 2015, a driverless car made a 373 mile road trip through France.

Scientists think that by 2050, almost all vehicles on the road will be autonomous, using cameras and sensors to guide and control them.

Automation could reduce the number of cars on the road, produce less emissions, cause less accidents, and ease traffic congestion.

BRILLIANT BODY

The human body is an incredible machine. From the strongest bones and muscles to the toughest teeth and fastest healing tissue, let's examine the intricate workings of all things human.

FOOD FACTORY

page 36

BONES AND MUSCLES

page 34

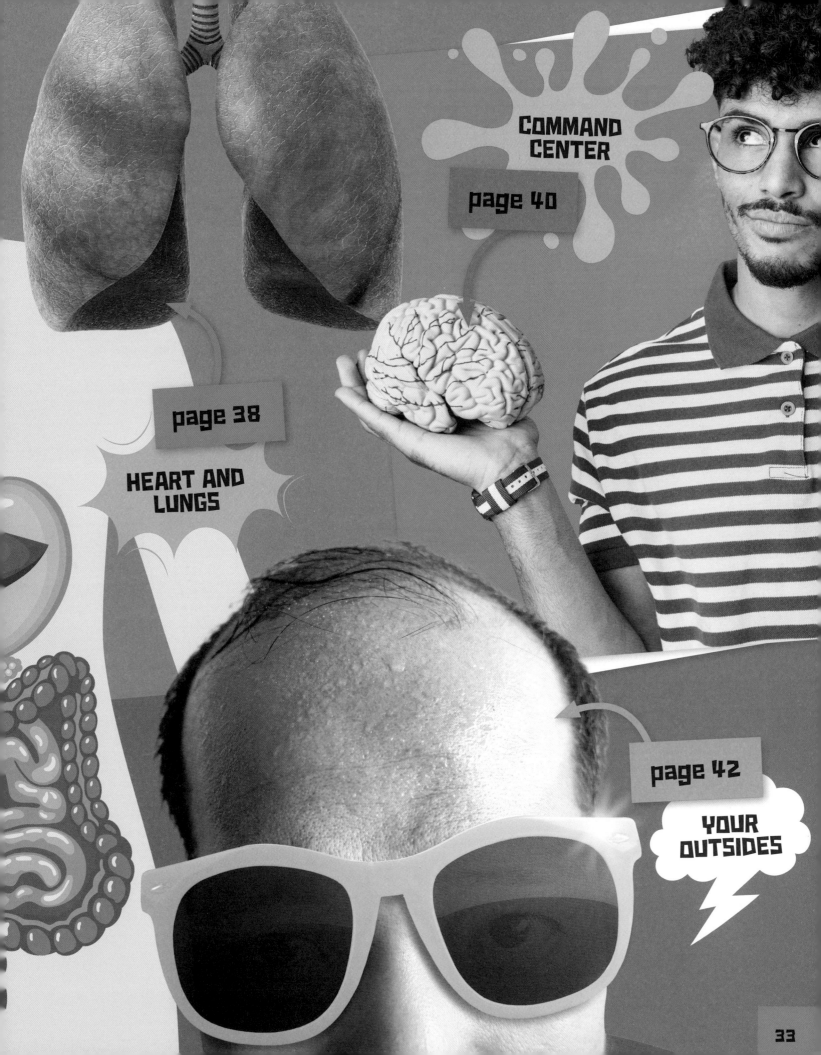

BONES AND MUSCLES

Without your bones and muscles, you'd be a shapeless blob!

Get a grip!

HANDS AND FEET

Did you know that half the bones in your body are found in your hands and feet?

Your feet keep you supported, balanced, and able to move, while your hands can perform intricate movements and have a tight grip.

With the right training, your fingers can even support your body weight, which is extra handy for rock climbers!

Babies are born with **300 bones.** Over time, some bones fuse together, leaving adults with **206.**

THE STRONG, INDEPENDENT FEMUR!

The femur (or thigh bone) is the longest and strongest bone in your body—it can support up to 30 times your body weight!

As a long bone, the inside of the femur is filled with soft marrow. This produces white and red blood cells, which protect your body from infection and carry vital oxygen to your body's cells.

STRONG BONES

Our bones are very light, but they're stronger than steel of the same weight.

NON-STOP MUSCLE

The hardest working muscle of all is your heart, and this never stops working throughout your entire life!

MIGHTY MUSCLES

Some muscles work without you knowing, such as those that help to digest your food and keep your heart beating.

The biggest muscle—in your backside—gives you support and helps you to walk upstairs, while the smallest muscles hold your inner ear together.

DID YOU KNOW?

There are over **600** muscles in your body, making up about **40** percent of your body weight.

WORKING HARD

It may seem strange, but standing still and doing nothing is tiring!

That's because your leg muscles are always adjusting to stop you falling over.

Your muscles are hard workers. You use 72 muscles to speak, 17 to smile, and 43 to frown! Just one step uses 200 muscles.

FOOD FACTORY

A deep dive into the digestive system!

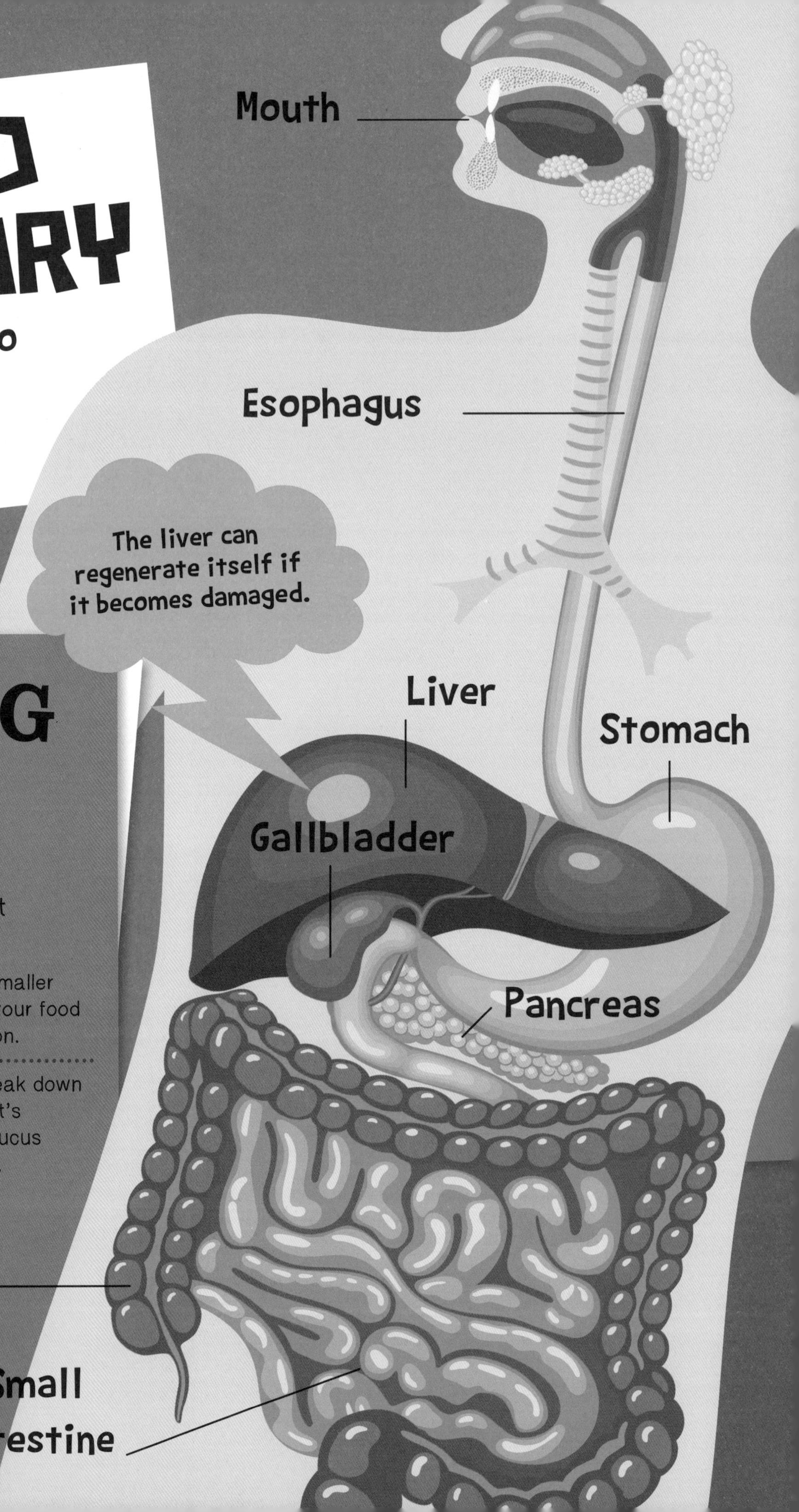

Mouth

Esophagus

The liver can regenerate itself if it becomes damaged.

AMAZING PARTS

Your digestive system is an amazing "factory line" food processor, which turns what you eat into you!

Your mouth chews your food into smaller pieces, but it also warms or cools your food to a better temperature for digestion.

Powerful stomach acid helps to break down your food but not your insides. That's because the stomach renews its mucus lining every two weeks to protect it.

Liver

Stomach

Gallbladder

Pancreas

Large intestine

Small intestine

ON THE MOVE

Your digestive system relies on involuntary muscle movements, called peristalsis, to move your food along.

In your food pipe (also known as your esophagus), these wave-like contractions push your food down into your stomach—even if you're upside down!

That's useful if you're an astronaut trying to eat and drink in space in zero gravity!

The movements continue through your small and large intestines, to keep everything flowing along.

I think my guts are confused!

GUT FEELING

Have you ever had butterflies or a sinking feeling in your stomach when you're worried or nervous?

This happens when blood is diverted from your stomach to your muscles and is an example of your "gut" telling your brain how you're feeling.

THE INTESTINE

The small intestine does over 90 percent of your body's digestive work.

It may only be about 23 foot long and under an inch wide, but lots of tiny folds and finger-like projections, called villi and microvilli, increase its surface area.

This large surface area helps your body to absorb as many nutrients from your food as possible, before it passes along to the large intestine as water and waste.

The surface area of the small intestine is roughly **2,690 square foot**. That's about the size of a tennis court!

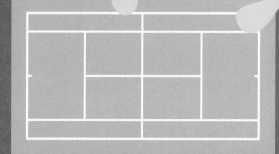

HEART AND LUNGS

This'll get your blood Pumping!

Your heart and lungs work together to give your body the oxygen rich blood it needs.

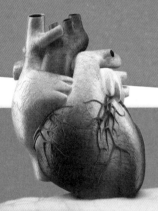

PUMP IT UP!

Your heart is about the size of a large fist.

The heartbeat you hear is the sound of the four valves in your heart opening and closing.

Every day, your heart beats over 100,000 times, pumping about 1,980 gallons of blood through arteries, veins, and capillaries.

LONG DISTANCE BLOOD VESSELS
If you stretched out your blood vessels end to end, they'd reach over **59,650 miles**, enough to travel around the world more than twice!

AMAZING ENERGY

When your muscles work hard, blood flow increases to give them the oxygen they need.

About 85 percent of your body heat comes from muscle contractions—that's why you shiver when your body needs to warm up!

Your heart generates enough energy each day to drive a truck over 18 miles. In a lifetime, it could get the truck to the Moon and back!

READY, SET, GO!
When your heart muscle pumps, it takes **16 seconds** for the blood to travel to your toes and back again.

DEEEEeP BREATHS

Like your small intestine, your lungs are much bigger than they look!

Right lung

Left lung

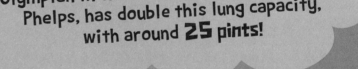

DID YOU KNOW
The average adult has a lung capacity of over **12 pints**, but the most successful Olympian in the world, US swimmer Michael Phelps, has double this lung capacity, with around **25 pints!**

Your left lung is slightly smaller than your right lung, to accommodate your heart.

If your lungs were opened out flat, they'd cover an area of over 2,000 square foot—that's at least 25 times the area of a king-size bed!

You breathe about 20,000 times a day, taking in about 2,900 gallons of air. This travels along 1,491 miles of airways to release oxygen into your bloodstream to reach the body parts that need it.

COMMAND CENTER

Your nervous system is an expert at communication ...

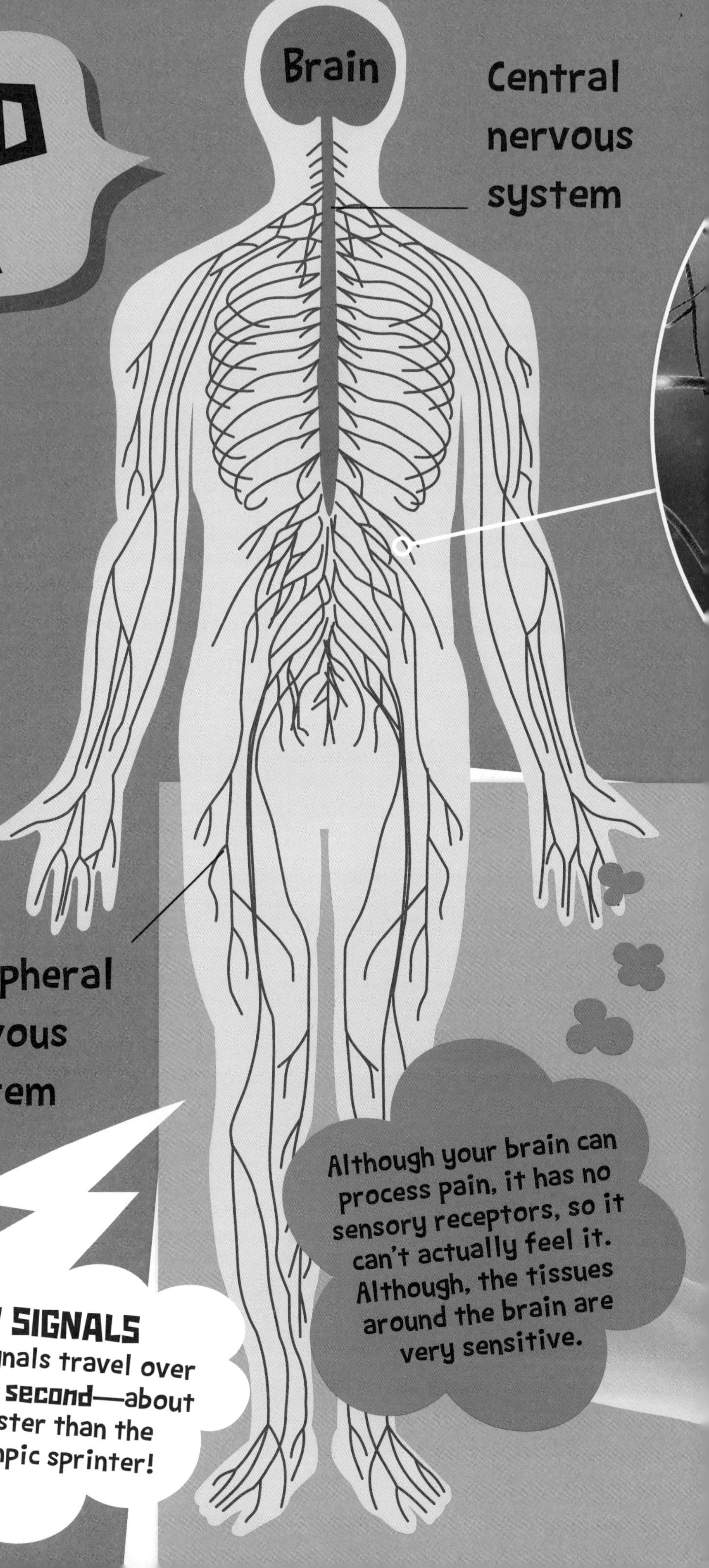

THE NERVOUS SYSTEM

Your body's nervous system controls how you think, feel, and move.

It also controls essential body processes, such as digestion, breathing, and blinking. It's made up of a huge network of neurons (nerve cells) that receive information and send signals to different parts of your body.

The central nervous system (your brain and spinal cord) works with your peripheral nervous system to tell your body what to do.

Brain

Central nervous system

Peripheral nervous system

SPEEDY SIGNALS
Some nerve signals travel over **328 feet per second**—about **10 times** faster than the fastest Olympic sprinter!

Although your brain can process pain, it has no sensory receptors, so it can't actually feel it. Although, the tissues around the brain are very sensitive.

SUPER STORAGE

Your body has billions of neurons. There are about 100 billion in your brain and about 100 million in your digestive system.

Scientists think the brain has almost unlimited storage capacity, with the possibility of 1,000 trillion neuron connections.

This one feels a little light!

If you lined up all your neurons, they'd stretch about **600 miles**, which is twice the length of the Grand Canyon!

THE BRAIN

An adult brain is about the size of two clenched fists and the weight of two basketballs.

When you're born, your brain is about a quarter of this size, but it more than doubles in size in the first year and is almost fully grown by the age of five.

The surface of your brain is covered with folds and crevices, which give it the surface area it needs to store information.

SENSATIONAL!

The longest nerve is the sciatic nerve, which stretches from your spinal cord to your toes, helping the muscles in your legs and feet to move, and giving them sensation.

Our fingertips are one of the most sensitive parts of our body. Each fingertip has more than 3,000 touch receptors that respond to pressure, pain, and other sensations.

DID YOU KNOW?
A brain can generate about **23 watts** of energy—enough to power a light bulb!

YOUR OUTSIDES

SWEATY STUFF You have about **200** sweat glands per square centimeter of skin, producing sweat that evaporates to cool your body's surface.

But hang on, we haven't even scratched the surface!

SUPPORTIVE SKIN

Your skin is your body's largest organ and can cover up to 21.5 square foot, which is about twice the size of a bath towel.

It protects your body from bacteria and helps to regulate your temperature.

Changes in blood flow to the skin can help to cool you down or warm you up. Your skin flushes when you exercise, for example, to keep you cool!

Is it hot in here?

HAIR-RAISING

Your hair is the fastest growing tissue in your body, and surprisingly strong!

Hair is made from keratin fibers—the same substance you find in your nails.

Although you lose about 100 hairs a day, the average head has over 100,000 hair follicles, so there's usually enough to keep things covered.

STRONG STUFF
A single hair can support a weight of up to **3.5 oz**, so a whole head of hair could theoretically support the weight of about two elephants!

EYE CATCHING

While a fingerprint has about 40 unique characteristics, your eye's iris has over 250! Iris recognition is now used as a more secure form of identification.

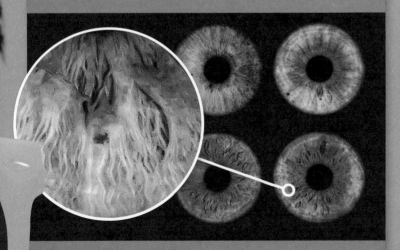

Your eyes can spot about a million different colors and have the fastest muscles in the body, which contract in less than 0.01 seconds.

The cornea is also the fastest healing tissue in the body, usually taking just 36 hours to repair a small scratch.

TOUGH TEETH

Tooth enamel is the hardest substance in your body.

LOOK AFTER THEM!
Tooth enamel is the only part of the body that can't repair itself.

It is made up of 96 percent minerals, mostly calcium and phosphorus.

It's harder than steel but it's more brittle and can break easily. The enamel can also be eroded by acids in your mouth, so it's important to clean your teeth regularly!

PAST TIMES

From fearsome rulers and brutal battles to amazing inventors and awe-inspiring record breakers. Let's turn back the clock to remember, with awe and horror, past events that have shaped our lives.

BLOODY BATTLES

From battlefields and aerial combat to wars at sea, history is full of gruesome conflict.

Wounded British troops await treatment at a medical station during the Battle of the Somme.

THE BATTLE OF THE SOMME

The first day of the Battle of the Somme, when the armies of Britain and France fought against the Germans, was one of the bloodiest days in history.

On 1 July 1916, nearly 20,000 Allied troops were killed, and another 37,000 were wounded—that's one soldier killed every 4.4 seconds.

The battle lasted **141 days**, resulting in more than a million casualties and over **300,000** lives lost.

THE BATTLE OF STALINGRAD

Fought between Germany and the Soviet Union, the Battle of Stalingrad was the biggest battle of the Second World War and one of the most brutal battles in history.

Stalingrad, on the Volga River in Russia, had important transport routes and access to oil fields. In August 1942, an attack by the Germans turned the city to rubble. But the Soviets counterattacked and surrounded the German army, forcing surrender.

DID YOU KNOW? In just five months, nearly **2 million** German and Soviet soldiers and civilians lost their lives.

Known as the Medal for the Defense of Stalingrad, this was awarded to Soviet soldiers who took part in the battle.

THE BATTLE OF SAINT-MIHIEL

One of the largest air battles took place in September 1918 toward the end of the First World War.

During the four day Battle of Saint-Mihiel, France and the US fought against the Germans both on the ground and in the air.

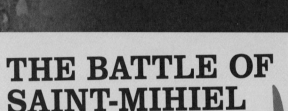

Nearly **1,500** Allied planes took on **500** German aircraft during the air battle.

Although the Allies lost 4,500 men during the land and air offensives, they took about 15,000 Germans prisoner.

THE BATTLE OF LEYTE GULF

The largest naval battle in history took place in the Philippines during the Second World War in October 1944.

The four day Battle of Leyte Gulf between Japan and the US spanned over 96,525 square miles.

The battle was the first time that the Japanese used kamikaze pilots against US warships. These pilots flew aircraft packed full of explosives on suicide missions, crashing them into enemy ships.

The Japanese and US lost 33 warships, 500 planes, and about 13,500 sailors and airmen between them during the battle.

A kamikaze plane hits a US warship.

ROTTEN RULERS

From Roman emperors to devilish dictators ...

You don't have to be mad to be emperor, but it helps!

HISTORY'S CRUELEST EMPEROR

The third Roman emperor Caligula (12–41 CE) was one of history's craziest rulers.

He was popular at first, but when he fell ill after 7 months, his behavior was so bad that people thought he was insane. He even tried to make his favorite horse a consul (political leader)!

Caligula was assassinated after just 4 years of power.

FAMILY FEUD

ON THE FIDDLE
Nero is said to have played his fiddle or harp while watching Rome burn.

If you thought Caligula was bad, things weren't much better with Nero (37–68 CE), the fifth Roman emperor. He was prone to execute anyone who didn't agree with him, including his own family!

Nero thought his mother was plotting against him, so he had her killed, and falsely accused his first wife Octavia of adultery to have her executed.

Many historians believe he burned down and completely destroyed Rome in nine days so he could rebuild it exactly how he wanted, although this is disputed.

IVAN THE TERRIBLE

Do I really look so terrible?

Russia's first ruler, or tsar, Ivan Vasilyevich (1530–1584), was another cruel, ruthless, and unpredictable ruler.

Ivan set up a secret police force and ordered the murder or assassination of anyone he distrusted, insisting they were cruelly tortured first.

When he suspected the leaders of the city of Novgorod to be plotting against him, he had the entire city destroyed.

Ivan killed his eldest son (and heir) by hitting him over the head with his scepter (a staff carried by rulers on special occasions).

DEATH AND DESTRUCTION

Adolf Hitler is one of the most despised leaders in history.

He started the Second World War in 1939 by invading Poland, and the resulting conflict led to around 60 million deaths.

Hitler also targeted Jewish people and other minorities and his concentration camps saw the death of around 11 million people, including 6 million Jewish people.

DID YOU KNOW?
There were more than **40** known assassination attempts on Hitler, before he took his own life in **1945.**

49

UNDERDOGS

Let's hear it for history's unsung heroes!

DNA is found in every cell in your body and is shaped like a spiral ladder.

ROSALIND FRANKLIN (1920–1958)

Rosalind Franklin developed an X-ray machine that revealed the structure of DNA, a genetic code found in plants and animals.

However, she died tragically young and was never recognized for her contribution. Franklin's colleague, Maurice Wilkins, showed the X-ray image to two Cambridge scientists, James Watson and Francis Crick, who published the research as their own!

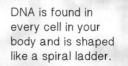

DID YOU KNOW?

Four years after Franklin's death from cancer, Watson, Crick, and Wilkins won the Nobel Prize for the DNA discovery.

You snooze, you lose!

ALFRED RUSSEL WALLACE (1823–1913)

The theory of evolution is attributed to Charles Darwin, but the theory was also proposed by English naturalist, Alfred Russel Wallace.

Alfred's name was overshadowed when Darwin published his book On the Origin of Species for the wider public.

During Wallace's travels in Asia, he realized that animals evolved because the fittest species survived and reproduced. He wrote to Darwin, who had already been working on the theory for over 20 years. The two men then worked together to put the proposal forward to the scientific establishment.

ADA LOVELACE (1815–1852)

British mathematician, Ada Lovelace, is now regarded as the world's first computer programmer)—100 years before computers were produced!

She was a huge fan of the first "calculating machines," and the first to recognize their ability to carry out large sequences of mathematical operations—aka, computer coding.

PROGRAMMING GENIUS
Ada's contributions to computer science were only discovered nearly **100 years** after her death.

THE TEAM BEHIND THE TELEPHONE

Alexander Graham Bell's design for a telephone was patented in 1876, but many other scientists played a part in the development of this technology.

Italian inventor, Antonio Meucci, began developing the idea of a talking telephone in 1849 and announced his invention in 1871 but he didn't have the funds to see it through.

Meanwhile, US engineer Elisha Gray tried to register an invention for a similar device on the same day as Bell—but it was too late! Talk about bad timing!

Meucci? Gray? Who?

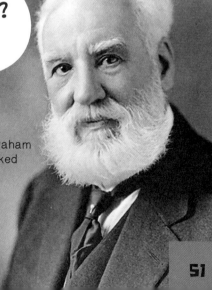

Alexander Graham Bell also worked on inventions for aircrafts and boats.

WAY, WAY BACK

Fun facts about the ancient past!

WEDGE WRITING
The Sumerians, like Kushim, wrote using cuneiform, a language with wedge-shaped symbols.

EARLY MAN

History is all about stories of people who lived long ago, but how far back does it date?

The first recorded name in history belonged to an accountant called Kushim who lived in Mesopotamia in around 3200 BCE. Kushim had used a tablet to record some business and signed his name at the bottom.

MISCHIEVOUS MASTER

Ancient Egyptian Pharaoh Pepi II Neferkare (2284–2216 BCE) had a sticky trick.

To stop himself being bothered by pesky flies, he ordered that other people in his court be covered in honey, to attract the flies instead!

SKILLED DESIGNERS

The Incas lived about 600 years ago and knew a thing or two about architecture.

Although their buildings were constructed without mortar (a type of cement to hold bricks together), they had an interlocking design that could survive earthquakes!

When the ground trembled, the stone walls would wobble, but tight connections returned them to their original place.

TIGHT FIT!
Inca building blocks fit so well together that you still can't push a sheet of paper between them.

Anyone know the date?

YEAR IN, YEAR OUT

Did you know the year 46 BCE was the longest year in human history—445 days!

Roman emperor Julius Caesar (100-44 BCE) wanted to change the Roman calendar to better fit the solar year.

The old calendar was based on the cycles of the Moon and was shorter than Caesar's new calendar which was based on the Sun. To make up the time, Caesar added 67 extra days to the year 46 BCE to transition to the new calendar.

LEAPING AHEAD
Caesar's new year had 12 months, most with 30 or 31 days, with an extra day added to the shorter month of February every 4 years, making a leap year.

ULTIMATE RECORDS

Some records ask to be broken, but these ones are going down in history . . .

I've got a head for heights!

SPACE JUMP

In 2012, daredevil parachutist Felix Baumgartner jumped from a capsule on the very edge of space, 25 miles above the ground!

The journey up took 90 minutes, but the jump down took just 10, with 4 minutes of freefall before his parachute opened.

To the relief of the world, Felix landed safely in New Mexico, USA.

LUCKY STRIKE

The chance of being struck by lightning is about 1 in 300,000, and the chance of being struck twice about 1 in 9 million!

But between 1942 and 1977, US park ranger, Roy Sullivan, was struck 7 times!

He suffered severe burns, and his hair was set on fire, but he miraculously survived.

Sullivan's nickname was the "spark ranger."

SUPERHUMAN SIZE

3593

Robert Wadlow was an average-sized baby, but his pituitary gland released an abnormally high level of human growth hormone that was never treated.

He outgrew his father by the age of 7 and at the time of his death, age 22, he was just under 9 feet tall!

DOUBLE MIRACLE

Tsutomu Yamaguchi was on a business trip to Hiroshima in 1945 when an atomic bomb blasted the city, instantly killing an estimated 80,000 people.

Yamaguchi was badly burned but somehow survived, returning to his hometown of Nagasaki, which was bombed three days later.

Yamaguchi slowly recovered from the aftereffects of the radiation and lived to the age of 93.

PRECIOUS PLANET

The wonders of Planet Earth are jaw-dropping. From scorching desert sands and snowcapped mountains to wild weather and danger zones. As we take a journey across the globe, prepare to be amazed by your surroundings!

EXTREME WEATHER

page 60

MAN-MADE WONDERS

page 58

MAN-MADE WONDERS

From hand carved sculptures to dizzying heights . . .

Moai statues on Easter Island.

How did I get here?

HEAVYWEIGHT HEAD
The heaviest Moai weighs **83.3 tons**, about the weight of **20 elephants**.

MYSTERIOUS MARVEL

The Moai statues of Easter Island, a remote volcanic island in the Pacific Ocean, are one of life's mysteries.

Carved between 1250 and 1500 CE, nearly 900 boulders sit across the landscape. Most are about 13 feet high, but the tallest finished statue stands just under 33 feet tall. It would have taken a lot of strength to move them!

THE GREAT WALL OF CHINA

The Great Wall of China is an enormous stone wall that was built to protect the country from invasion.

It took over 2,000 years to construct it and it stretches over 12,400 miles. The most visible part today is just under 5,000 miles long and was built during the period when China was controlled by rulers of the Ming Dynasty (1368–1644).

DID YOU KNOW?
If the wall was stretched out into a straight line, it would stretch half way around the world.

TIGER'S NEST

In 1692, the king of Bhutan built a beautiful monastery to commemorate the arrival of the Buddhist religion to his country.

The Taktsang Palphug Monastery (or "Tiger's Nest") is a sacred site built precariously on the steep cliffs of a Himalayan mountainside. It sits 10,236 feet above sea level and takes two hours to hike there over steep terrain.

The original structure burnt down in 1998, but it has been rebuilt in the traditional style.

DON'T LOOK DOWN!

If that doesn't give your head a spin, try the world's tallest outdoor elevator.

Built into the side of a huge cliff face in China, the Bailong Elevator ("hundred dragons elevator") opened in 2002. Over 1,050 feet tall, the upper section spans 561 feet above ground, giving a spectacular view. 65 Chinese yuan (China's currency) can get you a one-way ticket. Up or down: which would you choose?

EXTREME WEATHER

Deadly and dangerous, it's more than a bit of rain!

DID YOU KNOW?
There's enough power unleashed in a single lightning bolt to fuel an entire small town for a day!

FLASH-TASTIC!

The largest lightning strike ever recorded extended a whopping 477 miles across Mississippi, Louisiana, *and* Texas in April 2020!

Blink and you'd have missed it, but it'd take you over 7 hours to drive that far in a fast car.

The longest lasting lightning flash hit Uruguay in the same year and lasted for 17 seconds!

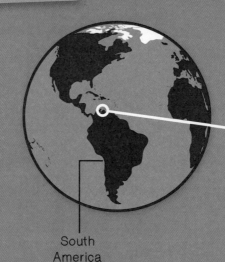

South America

Lake Maracaibo

The largest hurricane on record, Typhoon Tip, struck Japan in 1979, with a diameter of over 1,243 miles. It caused over 600 mudslides across the country, and was so big, it was classed as a "super typhoon."

In 2015, Hurricane Patricia became the fastest tropical cyclone ever recorded, with winds blowing over 200 mph—that's the speed of a race car!

Typhoon Tip 1979 1,243 miles

WILD WINDS

In 1972, tree-flinging winds and a brutal blizzard buried 200 Iranian villages under 26 foot of snow for an entire week!

In 1989, a 1 mile wide tornado hit speeds of over 150 mph and tore through cities in Bangladesh along a path 9 times longer than the height of Mount Everest!

26 foot

26 foot of snow is the equivalent of one and a half times the height of a giraffe.

THE NEVER-ENDING STORM

Along Venezuela's Catatumbo River, which flows into Lake Maracaibo, 28 lightning strikes occur every minute for 9 hours a day, 150 days a year!

The only time it has paused was during a 2010 drought, when no lightning struck for four months. The storm is raging today and scientists still don't understand why!

FIRE WHIRLS

They're what you get when you cross almighty winds with intense, burning heat.

And they're just as terrifying as they sound. A fire whirl's burning core sucks up debris into a flame-spitting vortex, reaching over 1,832 °F!

In 2017, one in New Zealand blasted 984 foot in the air—about three times as high as London's Big Ben!

HOT 'N' COLD

From hot, arid deserts to frozen ice fields ...

IT'S A SCORCHER!

Death Valley, Colorado, USA, is the hottest place on Earth.

When the Sun warms the rocks and soil there, the heat becomes trapped in the steep-sided valley. Record temperatures during the day have reached 130 °F, and summer nighttime temperatures often exceed 86 °F!

CLEVER CREATURES

While air conditioning and swimming pools are a relief to the humans in Death Valley, many animals have adapted to live there.

COOL BUNNY
The desert hare has unusually large ears to help it release heat and stay cool.

FREEZING CONDITIONS

Brrrrrrrrrrr!

Vostok Research Station in Antarctica is the coldest and driest place on Earth.

The air is so cold it can damage your lungs, so research scientists wear masks to warm the air first. The research station is constantly buried under a 10 foot layer of snow, and workers dig out the entrance every summer.

Now that's how you stay cool!

Kangaroo rats don't need to drink. They just rely on their food for moisture and produce concentrated urine and dry feces. While roadrunner birds can lower their body temperature on cold desert nights to save energy.

ICY WORLD

Many animals have adapted to live in Antarctic conditions, with a thick layer of blubber under their skin to keep warm, and layers of fur or feathers.

Colonies of penguins huddle together to keep warm, and their bodies keep their small flippers and feet at a lower temperature to reduce heat loss.

TOP TO BOTTOM

From the tallest peaks to the deepest dungeons ...

TOP OF THE WORLD

It takes about 40 days to climb Mount Everest, Earth's tallest peak.

You could climb it quicker, but your body needs time to adjust to the changes of altitude, as oxygen levels at the top are only a third of what they are at sea level, making it very hard to catch your breath!

CRAZY CLIMBERS!
Kamil Rita Sherpa has climbed the mountain 24 times. Lakpa Gelu Sherpa reached the summit in a record of 10 hours and 56 minutes!

MOUNTAIN RIVER

The Son Doong ("Mountain River") Cave in Vietnam is so big it has its own river and rainforest.

With some parts reaching over 650 feet tall and 574 foot wide, it could fit a block of 40 story skyscrapers. The cave also stretches for almost 6 miles.

GATES OF HELL

A fiery glow can be seen from miles around in Turkmenistan.

In the 1970s, a sinkhole collapsed in a natural gas field there, releasing dangerous methane gas. To get rid of the gas, the Soviet government set fire to the crater, in the hope it would burn itself out. But this didn't exactly go to plan …

Mount Everest is 29,032 foot tall, which is just below the cruising height of a passenger jet!

FIERY GATES
The crater has been burning for 50 years!

You don't want to go in there!

TOXIC HOLE

Perhaps one of the most inhospitable places on Earth is Movile Cave, 66 feet underground in Romania.

Accidentally discovered in the 1980s, this 20-foot-deep cavern is pitch black and full of toxic gases. Cut off for nearly 5 million years, scientists have found over 30 previously unknown species of worms, shrimps, and other creatures living there and feeding on bacteria.

WATERY WORLD

From boiling rivers and steep steps to raging oceans and pink lagoons.

THE PINK LAKE

Lakes are usually green, brown or blue, but Australia is home to over 10 vibrant pink ones!

The most famous, Lake Hillier, stays a bubblegum pink all year. This is caused by bacteria and algae that thrive in the salty water.

Although they're technically safe to swim in, it's not advisable due to both their high salt content and the desire to protect the lakes.

SALTY WATER
The water in Lake Hillier is **10 times** saltier than seawater.

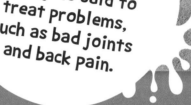

STUNNING STEPS

Iran is home to a beautiful natural staircase of water pools, sitting on a rust-colored bed of limestone.

Badab-e Surt was created over thousands of years as hot springs trickled down the mountainside. The water cooled, leaving behind deposits that hardened to give the slope a terraced edge.

Water from the springs is said to treat problems, such as bad joints and back pain.

BOILING WATERS

Imagine being told stories about a mythical boiling river deep in the jungle—and growing up to find it for yourself!

This is what happened to Peruvian geophysicist, Andrés Ruzo, who discovered the "La Bomba" tributary of the Amazon River where the water is heated by geothermal springs to 203 °F!

SWIM IF YOU DARE!
Some people swim in the river, but only once heavy rainfall has diluted the temperature.

DEVIL'S TRIANGLE

The Bermuda Triangle in the North Atlantic Ocean is famously feared. It's a place where over 50 ships and 20 aircraft have been lost in mysterious circumstances.

It's said there are over 300 sunken boats on the seabed, and in some parts 4 shipwrecks lie on top of each other!

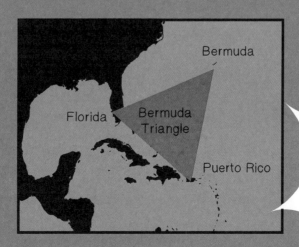

Bermuda

Florida

Bermuda Triangle

Puerto Rico

Today, we know the area has a network of reefs that could break a wooden ship apart, as well as sudden storms.

AWESOME ANIMALS

The animal kingdom is full of curious creatures, and record breakers, too! From giant ocean dwellers and tiny terrors to super senses and vicious venom. Let's celebrate the diversity of the animal world.

page 70

page 72

WAIT! THAT'S REAL?

WILD WEIRDOS!

Animals that could be pulled straight from a fairy tale ... or nightmare!

WAIT! THAT'S REAL?

DRAGON'S BREATH

Komodo dragons are brutal predators with a lethal (and gross) biting attack.

When hunting, they rely on camouflage to ambush prey three times their size. They inflict a vicious bite, then let germs and venom from their saliva slowly seep into their prey.

LIVING DINOSAUR?
They have very similar skulls to the mosasaur, a huge, extinct aquatic reptile.

Komodo dragons weigh up to **135 kg** (the same as a female grizzly bear).

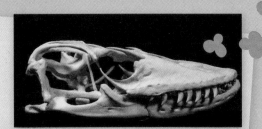

SAILOR SIGHT

Sailors in the 15th century believed that manatees were actually mermaids!

Unlike mermaids, however, they weigh as much as 1,323 lbs (the equivalent to 6 baby elephants) and grow to 10 foot (the length of 2 park benches). Today, they are often referred to as "sea cows" ... hardly as flattering, poor things.

WONDROUS WHALE

Is there anything more unbelievable than an underwater unicorn?

Narwhals are small whales with giant tusks sprouting through their lips—just like unicorn horns! The tusks are filled with millions of nerve endings, which scientists think help narwhals to navigate during migration.

DID YOU KNOW?
Narwhal tusks can grow up to **10 foot**—as long as a diving board.

SEA TERROR!

Legends tell of the Kraken: an enormous, tentacled sea monster that dragged ships to the bottom of the ocean ...

Sightings of the giant squid are rare and they are hardly ever caught on camera!

Giant squid can grow up to **43 foot** (as long as a bus).

43 foot

Surely, they can't be real? With eyes up to 12 inches across, introducing ... the giant squid! While stories of squid attacks on ships probably aren't true, scars from their huge suckers are often found on the skin of sperm whales!

WILD WEIRDOS!

The animal world is full of surprises ...

Who are you calling big nose?

HOW MANY OCTOPUSES DOES IT TAKE TO UNSCREW A JAR?

I'm smarter than I look!

Just one! Octopuses are highly intelligent creatures, with nine brains—one between the eyes and one in each arm.

The arms can work independently, making them excellent multi-taskers.

They've been known to build their own dens from stones, to guide an arm through a maze to find food, and yes, they can even work out how to unscrew a jar!

ANCHOVIES

LEECH-A-LOT

They may be small, slimy creatures, but leeches make up for their size.

They have a brain in each of their 32 body segments, as well as 2 hearts, 10 stomachs, 5 pairs of eyes, and 3 jaws, each with about 100 teeth!

GROSS FACT ALERT!
Leeches can grow up to 5-10 times their normal size when they feast on your blood.

SUPER SENSES

Our senses help to navigate the world around us, but some animals do things differently!

The proboscis monkey has an enormous nose—but not for smelling! Scientists think it's used as an echo chamber so the monkey's call impresses females and warns off rival males.

Butterflies have taste receptors on their feet to identify edible substances. Imagine that!

There's no hiding from a slow loris. Its huge eyes allow it to see in almost complete darkness!

A chameleon's tongue is about twice the size of its body.

Lobsters have sensitive hairs on their pincers.

STRANGE SMILES

It's not just the size of some tongues that are odd!

Snakes and lizards smell with their tongues, but the tongue of the Komodo dragon can detect rotting flesh up to 5 miles away!

And beware the freshwater pacu fish in South America or the sheepshead fish on American coasts—their humanlike teeth, used to crack nuts, shells, or fruit, are a little unnerving!

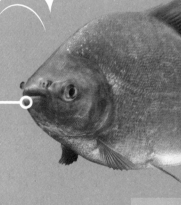

A giraffe's tongue is over 3 foot long.

A blue whale's tongue can weigh almost as much as an elephant!

DARLING BUT DEADLY

Some of Earth's cutest creatures have a dark side, too.

BEWARE THE BEARS

Panda bears and polar bears may look cute and cuddly, but they're some of the most dangerous creatures on Earth.

Pandas are vegetarian so they don't hunt humans, but can turn nasty if they feel threatened. Their sharp teeth and claws can be deadly.

No hugs, Please!

DON'T TOUCH!

Beware the golden poison frog. This creature may look cute, but one touch and you're a goner!

No larger than a bottle cap, the skin secretions of this frog have enough poison to kill 10 adults! Native tribes in the Colombian rainforests use the poison to coat the tips of their blow darts when they go hunting.

DID YOU KNOW? The fire-bellied snake is the only snake that eats the frog because it is immune to its poison.

BLOWFISH BALL GAMES

The blowfish (or pufferfish) is another deadly creature. It has enough poison in its body to kill 30 adults!

With their long bodies and bulbous heads, blowfish can't swim that well so they're an easy target for predators.

When they feel threatened, they take in lots of water to turn themselves into a spiky ball (not at all appetizing!).

TOXIC TREAT! Blowfish body organs are toxic to any predator brave enough to take a bite.

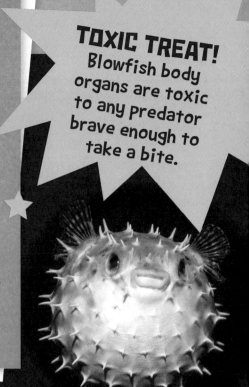

BLUE RING OF TERROR!

Stunning but savage, the blue ring octopus can be found among the coral reefs and rock pools of the Pacific and Indian Ocean coasts.

Its body is tiny—about 1.5 inches across—but packs enough venom to kill 26 adults!

When threatened, bright blue rings appear on its body as a warning and its almost painless bite injects its deadly venom.

Polar bears are meat eaters, so they'd have no qualms about attacking a human, especially if food is scarce.

They have a keen sense of smell, and one swipe of their powerful paw could take your arm off.

DID YOU KNOW? A polar bear's claws can measure **4 inches** long!

ACTUAL SIZE!

4 inches

LIMBS GALORE

Tentacles or legs, these guys have them all ... literally.

FAST MOVER!
All those legs help centipedes run incredibly fast, at about **16 in a second!**

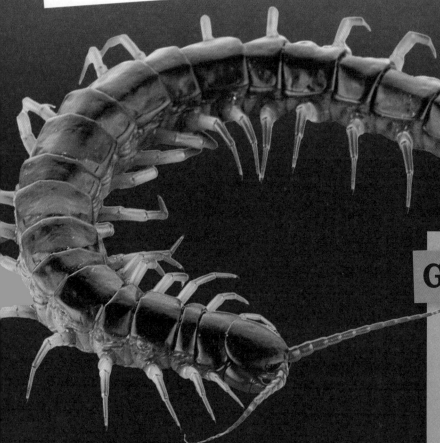

GIANT TIGER PRAWN

The giant tiger prawn is named after its distinctive black and orange coloring and is widely farmed for food.

Reaching 12 inches in length, it can swim as well as scuttle across the seabed with its 5 pairs of legs.

Weighing up to 10.6 oz—about the weight of 2 large hamsters—these big boys are most at home in warm Asian waters.

CENTIPEDE

You'd be forgiven for thinking a centipede has 100 legs, but depending on the species, some have less than 20 or more than 300!

Centipedes have legs on the sides of every segment of their body (always an odd number), as well as two venomous pincers for protection and to catch their insect prey.

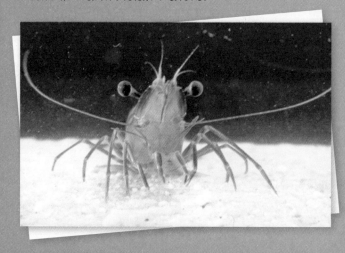

GIANT HUNTSMAN SPIDER

If you're afraid of spiders, your worst nightmare would be the giant huntsman spider, from Laos.

They are so fast, they don't need to build webs to catch their prey, they just prowl around for their next victim and inject a venomous bite.

ACTUAL SIZE!

I've got more legs than you!

MILLIPEDE

In 2021, a new species of millipede was found to have the most legs of any creature on Earth—1,300!

Found in an Australian mining area, 197 feet below Earth's surface, the millipedes are about 4 inches long and less than a quarter of an inch wide.

They live in total darkness and use their sense of smell and touch to get around.

PROTECTIVE BALL
Millipedes protect themselves by curling into a tight coil.

DEEP-SEA CREATURES

Some sea creatures reach ginormous sizes. The lower you go, the weirder it gets . . .

A blue whale's heart is the size of a small car, and a child could crawl along its aorta blood vessel! You can hear its heart beat from around **2 miles** away.

THE BLUE WHALE

The Antarctic blue whale is the world's largest animal, reaching up to 98 foot in length, about 2.5 buses, and weighing up to 168 tons, which is nearly 40 elephants!

Jellyfish tentacles can reach **121 foot long** while its body is only around **6.5 foot wide**.

LION'S MANE JELLYFISH

The long flowing tentacles of the lion's mane jellyfish make it one of Earth's longest creatures.

It may look a beautiful sight, but its tentacles have a powerful sting, even when they're not attached to its body! That's bad news for any fish in the vicinity.

GIANT PACIFIC OCTOPUS

Like the giant squid (see page 71), the giant Pacific octopus is a big beast, with arms stretching 33 feet, and weighing about 110 lbs.

Found off the coast of Alaska, Japan, and the USA, this reddish-pink creature camouflages itself when it feels threatened.

A female will lay up to 74,000 eggs the size of rice grains, and watch over them for seven months.

Just before the eggs hatch, the mother will die—sometimes alarmingly, by eating her own arms!

RIBBONFISH

Living in the deep sea is "oar-some!"

The ribbonfish is the world's longest bony fish. It can grow up to 36 foot long!

YUCK!
Apparently, the flesh of the ribbonfish is flabby and gooey— not good to eat!

The ribbonfish can also weigh more than 550 lbs, or about the weight of a large pig.

It lives 3,280 foot deep in dark ocean waters and rarely comes to the surface.

With its large eyes, it's often described as a sea serpent or dragon, and its long oar-like fins have given it the nickname "oarfish."

DEADLY DINOSAURS

From terrifying talons and razor-sharp teeth to powerful jaws and breakneck speeds, let's travel back in time to explore the lives of these prehistoric beasts.

page 82

CARNIVORES

HERBIVORES

page 84

page 86

OMNIVORES

page 88

MONSTERS
OF THE
DEEP

page 90

POWERFUL
FLIGHT

SPINELESS
SURVIVORS

page 92

CARNIVORES

The most terrifying dinosaurs had a taste for meat ... and only meat.

BRAIN POWER

Beware the meat-eating dinosaurs!

With a larger brain in proportion to their body size, meat-eaters were much more intelligent than their plant-eating cousins. They were fast and agile, with quick reflexes, and keen senses. They often hunted in packs, communicating with each other to track and trap their prey.

Being a dinosaur isn't all plain sailing!

TYRANNOSAURUS REX

DID YOU KNOW?
Each T. rex tooth was about **8 inches long.**

The T. rex is perhaps the most famous meat-eater of all.

Its razor-sharp, serrated teeth, and phenomenal bite strength meant it could easily crunch through bone as well as meat.

With its powerful legs and extraordinary sense of smell, you wouldn't want to get caught close to this one!

SPINOSAURUS

The largest meat-eater was spinosaurus. It was 46 foot long and weighed up to 9 tons!

Spinosaurus liked to hunt in rivers as well as on land, making it a doubly dangerous predator! It had a crocodile-like skull with nostrils positioned high up so it could breathe when partially submerged in water. Powerful limbs and a strong tail helped it to propel forward and swim fast.

UTAHRAPTOR

But perhaps the fiercest meat-eater of all was the utahraptor.

In 1991, the first utahraptor was found in Utah, USA. It had 12-inch killer claws that could gut its prey easily. Up to 10 foot tall and 26 foot long, this intelligent creature could dash, dodge and leap up to 16 foot in the air to attack. You'd be sorry your paths had crossed!

HERBIVORES

The plant-eating dinosaurs were slow, but strong!

GENTLE GIANTS

Some of the largest dinosaurs ate plants, and they had to eat a bus-sized pile of greenery a day to sustain their size!

They often lived in herds and many had spikes and horns to defend themselves from predators.

ARMORED DINO
Ankylosaurus had bony plates studded with spikes all over its body and a huge bony club at the end of its tail.

DID YOU KNOW?
Kosmoceratops had 15 sharp horns around its face.

With their long necks, titanosaurs could reach trees the height of a six-story building.

How's the weather down there?

115 foot

TITANOSAURS

The largest land animals that have ever lived are known as the titanosaurs.

Some of the largest fossil finds in Argentina include the titanosaurs argentinosaurus and patagotitan. These fossils point to creatures more than 115 foot long and weighing more than 67 tons.

STOMACH STONES
Some herbivores had stones stored in their stomachs called "gastroliths." They helped grind their food so it was easier to digest.

GOOD DIGESTION

Herbivores had flat teeth to strip leaves from trees and grind plant matter into a pulp.

Some, like the duck-billed hadrosaurs with over 1,000 teeth in their powerful jaws, were particularly good at grinding leaves and twigs.

In one seismosaurus fossil, over 240 gastroliths were found, with some as large as a grapefruit.

SLOW LIVING
The stegosaurus is often ridiculed for its lime-sized brain, which was rather small for its van-sized body!

The pointy plates along its back and tail were good for attracting a mate or warding off predators. Some scientists think they might have helped to regulate its body temperature, too.

OMNIVORES

Meat or veggies, omnivores weren't picky at dinner time!

ORNITHOMIMIDS

About **1-2 percent** of dinosaurs ate both plants and meat, which helped them survive in a variety of habitats. Some of the fastest dinosaurs were omnivores.

Ornithomimids were very similar to today's ostriches and could run as fast as a greyhound!

They used their long tail for balance when they made a dash from predators, and their arms and claws were good for gathering plants, seeds, and small prey, as well as digging for grubs.

EGG EATERS

Oviraptors used their powerful beaks to break shellfish or dinosaur eggs.

POWERFUL JAWS

Omnivores are easily identifiable from their varied teeth, shaped to deal with tough meat or chewy twigs. But some had no teeth at all! Instead, they used scissor-like beaks to tear their food and their strong jaws to crush it.

TROODONTIDS

Troodontids were some of the smallest dinosaurs, measuring about 12–16 inches long.

They had a long skull with up to 100 serrated teeth which they used to puncture and pull at their prey.

Their feet had a retractable claw on their second toe which gave them excellent grip.

Troodontids had huge eyes set toward the front of their face, giving them binocular vision—useful for spotting prey!

DEINOCHEIRUS

In 1965, a pair of giant arms, each around 95 inches long, were found in Mongolia's Gobi Desert. Each arm had a terrifying three-fingered hand with claws.

Some thought it might belong to a monster even more ferocious than the T. rex, but over 40 years later, additional bones suggested it was an ostrich-type dinosaur that only fed on plants and fish.

About 16 foot tall and 33 foot long, deinocheirus had a long, narrow skull, with a wide toothless bill.

MONSTERS OF THE DEEP

While dinosaurs mainly ruled the land, marine reptiles were king of the oceans.

DINNER TIME!
In 2020, the fossil of a 16-foot ichthyosaur found in China had the remains of a 13-foot creature in its belly, which it had swallowed whole!

ICHTHYOSAURS

Weighing up to 90 tons, with a skull the size of a small car, ichthyosaurs were the largest marine reptile known to man.

New fossil evidence suggests they could have grown up to 115 foot in length—surpassing the blue whale!

Megalodon teeth have been found all over the world, with some measuring nearly **8 in** long.

LIOPLEURODON

It's difficult to find the complete remains of large prehistoric creatures because scavengers often disturb decomposing body parts and erosion wears some of the bones away.

But in Mexico in 2002, scientists found a complete skeleton of a liopleurodon with spinal bones upto 12 inches long! With its double-bed-sized skull and teeth up to 10 inches long, its jaws were thought to be powerful enough to chew through granite.

DID YOU KNOW?
Some marine reptiles gave birth to live young. In 2014, scientists found the fossil of an ichthyosaur giving birth to 3 offspring.

MEGALODON

Another feared sea creature, the megalodon was 30 times bigger than today's great white shark!

It reached lengths of around 60 feet and had a bite 3 times stronger than a T. rex. When its jaws were open, it could have swallowed 2 human adults standing side by side!

POWERFUL FLIGHT

Even the skies were filled with giants!

WINGED REPTILES

At the time of the dinosaurs, pterosaurs ruled the skies, though they weren't technically dinosaurs themselves.

Rather like the bats we see today, pterosaur wings were flaps of skin attached to a very long fourth finger.

They used these wings to soar through the sky, but fossilized footprints suggest they walked on all fours, too.

DID YOU KNOW?
Scientists think pterosaurs folded their wing finger upward to walk on their hands and feet.

QUETZALCOATLUS

The biggest pterosaur, quetzalcoatlus, was the largest known animal to take flight, and had a wingspan of up to 43 foot—the size of a small plane!

DID YOU KNOW?
Large pterosaurs could fly nonstop for about 10 days, covering around **10,000 miles.** They could easily cross an ocean, thanks to their light, hollow bones, strong muscles, and powerful hind limbs.

43 foot

This carnivorous creature had a giant, 7-foot-long toothless beak. Scientists think this beak could have been used to either swoop down to snatch prey, or probe through sand to find fish, crabs, and worms.

ARAMBOURGIANIA

In the 1990s, scientists realized that a fossil previously identified as a pterosaur wing finger was in fact an incomplete, 20-foot-long neck bone belonging to the arambourgiania!

It's believed that their entire neck could in fact grow over 10 foot long, making the creature as tall as a giraffe!

SPINELESS SURVIVORS

Invertebrates are animals without backbones, and they dominated the ancient world.

Invertebrate life **500 million years ago** was extremely diverse and ranged from tiny, microscopic organisms to huge, coiled shells more than **7 foot** across.

ANCIENT ORGANISMS

Today, about 97 percent of all the animals on Earth are invertebrates, like worms and insects.

Until about 500 million years ago, however, no animals had a backbone!

We know a lot about these ancient creatures from their fossils, including what they ate, how they hunted, and what Earth was like when they were alive.

SHOCK DISCOVERY

In 2018, the fossil of the largest known land-based invertebrate was found in Northumberland, England. It was a car-sized millipede called arthropleura!

Scientists think the creature lived about 300 million years ago.

The millipede has been estimated to have a total length of 8 foot and to be about the weight of a large dog.

8 foot

TOUGH COOKIES

Tardigrades are the toughest creatures on (and off) the planet.

They've been around for at least half a billion years already and have survived 5 mass extinctions.

Also known as "water bears" or "moss piglets," these tiny creatures—about a tenth of an inch long—can even go a year without food or water.

LESSONS FROM THE PAST

Tiny marine organisms called foraminifera (or "forams") have also been around as long as the tardigrades.

About the size of the period on this page, their fossilized remains are incredibly valuable to scientists.

They reveal secrets about Earth's past climate and environmental conditions, how life reacted to those conditions, and help us to predict how best to cope and adapt to future climate change.

I'm also good under pressure!

INDESTRUCTIBLE!
From **-457 °F** to over **302 °F**, they don't mind freezing or boiling conditions and can survive exposure to the vacuum of space.

INDEX

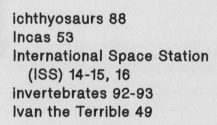

ACKNOWLEDGMENTS

The publishers would like to thank the following sources for their kind permission to reproduce the pictures in this book.
The page numbers for each of the photographs are listed below, giving the page on which they appear in the book and any location indicator
(c-center, t-top, b-bottom, l-left, r-right).
11cr courtesy of NASA, 47b courtesy of US Navy, 3br, 48 courtesy of the Metropolitan Museum of Art, 61b courtesy of US Fish and Wildlife Service
Creative Commons:
22t Clfeider, 31br Dllu, 45tl Nirmaljk, 76b Materialscientist
Shutterstock.com:
1b Dotted Yeti, 2 Andrew Harker, 3tl Nazarii_Neshcherenskyi, 3tcl Dima Zel, 3tr ArtEvent ET, 3bc adike, 4tc Pisut chounyoo, 4tr Elenarts, 4bl Travel Stock,
4bc Seregraff, 4br ExpressionImage, 5tc Pisut chounyoo, 5tr Elenarts, 5bl Vixit, 5bc Seregraff, 5br ExpressionImage, 6-7t, 10t Pavel Chagochkin, 6bl, 8-9c
Lukasz Pawel Szczepanski and Real Illusion, 6-7b, 14-15c Artsiom P, 7tr, 12-13b PlanilAstro, 7br, 17br M.Aurelius, 8bc peipeiro, 9tr Artsiom P, 9cr Antony
McAulay,9cl MarcelClemens, 9br artyway, 11t muratart, 11c Nazarii_Neshcherenskyi, 11b Kit Leong, 12-13t Denis Belitsky, 14bl Miguel Angel LG, 15tr
joshimerbin, 15cl Dima Zel, 16c tutti_frutti, 16b woverwolf, 17t Merlin74, 17tr fukume, 18bl, 23tr nobeastsofierce, 18br, 25t catwalker, 19t, 26-27 Damir Khabirov
and Limbitech, 19bl, 28t Andrew Harker, 19br, 31t andrey_l, 20t lunamarina, 21tl stockphoto mania, 21tr Evan Lorne, 23cl Maxim999, 24 Anton Gvozdikov,
25cr Zapp2Photo, 25bl MikeDotta, 25br Clive Stapleton, 27br Supamotionstock.com, 28b Andrey_Popov, 29t IgorZh, 29b Andrey Suslov, 30-31t Keith Tarrier,
32r, 36 Olga Bolbot, 32bl, 34-35b Thorsten Schmitt, 33tl, 39tr LYW, 33tr, 41br Krakenimages.com, 33b, 42b Boyloso, 34t Vitalii Matokha, 34cl and bl, 35tl
SciePro, 35c Peddalanka Ramesh Babu, 35r adike, 37tl Dee-sign, 37tr dwi putra stock, 38 Luis Molinero, 39cl AnyaPL, 39bl Pheelings media, 40r Systemoff,
41tl MattLphotography, 41bl Snezhana_G, 43tr JRP Studio, 43bl MT-R, 43bc Atomazul, 44tr, 51c gillmar and HappySloth, 44bl, 46 Everett Collection, 45tl,
50br gillmar, 45tr, 53b Svetlana Pasechnaya, 45b, 54cl LeBlancStudio, 47t ArtEvent ET, 49tl Kraft74, 50t vitstudio, 51tr gillmar, 52t Volha Valadzionak, 52b
Kovaleva_Ka and Nadzin, 53tr Erika Cristina Manno, 54-55b Macrovector, 55t Riddick Patrec, 56bl, 58l Stefano73, 56-57b, 65c Antonin Vinter, 57t, 63t MP
cz, 57br, 66t matteo_it, 59t aphotostory, 59bl Khanthachai C, 59br WAN CHEUK NANG, 60t Vasin Lee, 60b ii-graphics, 62t Lucky-photographer and Alex
Bascuas, 63bl Been there YB, 63br vladsilver, 64-65b Vixit, 64-65br David A Knight, 65bl rogelson, 65br M-Production, 67tr Jakob Fischer, 67cl Ioana_art,
67b WindVector, 68bl, 70tl Patrick Rolands, 68br, 73tr Seregraff, 69tl, 74t Thorsten Spoerlein, 69tr, 77t iSKYDANCER, 69b, 79cl Kondratuk Aleksei, 70bl IHX,
70br Anna Kucherova, 70tl Greg Amptman, 71bl Kletr, 72t Yusnizam Yusof, 72bl ennar0, 72br socrates471, 73tc Butterfly Hunter, 73c Bildagentur Zoonar
GmbH, 73cl Holger Kirk, 73cr NAPA, 73bc David Jara Bogunya, 73bl Maria Spb, 73br Ammit Jack, 74bl V-yan, 74-75b ILYA AKINSHIN, 75tr Pete Niesen,
75cl rudy tulang, 76t SUCHARUT CHOUNYOO, 77b Pisut chounyoo, 78-79t bekirevren, 78br maikbrand, 79b Dotted Yeti, 80bl, 83t ExpressionImagem,
80-81b, 85br PixelSquid3d, 81tl, 87b Elenarts, 81tr, 89t SciePro, 81cr, 91t Elenarts, 81br, 93br Dotted Yeti, 82t Daniel Eskridge, 82-83b Herschel Hoffmeyer,
83cr Warpaint, 84l YuRi Photolife, 84br Warpaint, 85t Warpaint, 85tl stockt0_0, 86t YuRi Photolife, 86br YuRi Photolife, 87t Catmando, 88-89 Daniel
Eskridge, 88br SEAN D THOMAS, 89br Warpaint, 90-91t Daniel Eskridge, 90b Daniel Eskridge, 91b Noiel, 92-93t Dotted Yeti, 92-93b Peddalanka Ramesh
Babu, 93tc Ralf Juergen Kraft, 94tr Andrew Harker, 94bl Lukasz Pawel Szczepanski, 95tr JRP Studio, 95br iSKYDANCER, 96t joshimerbin

Every effort has been made to acknowledge correctly and contact the source and/or copyright holder of each picture. Any unintentional errors or omissions
will be corrected in future editions of this book.

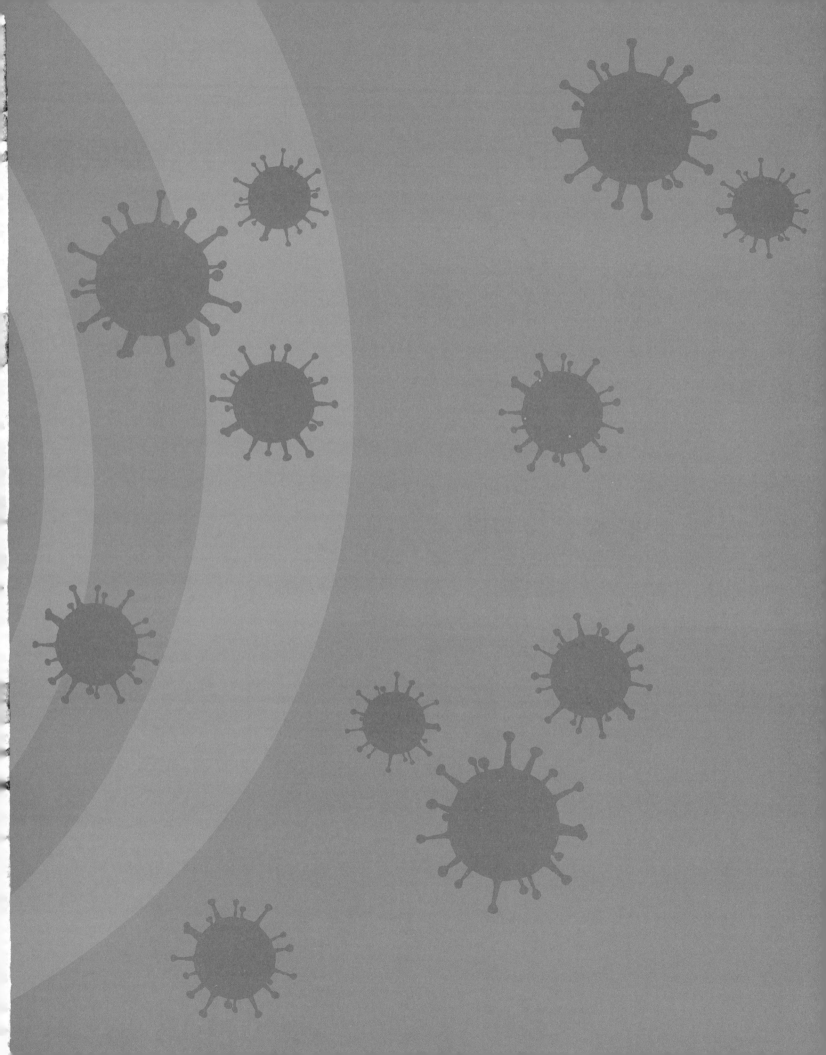